Giovanni Battista
BONONCINI

(1670 – 1747)

Divertimento da camera III
for Treble (Alto) Recorder and Basso continuo
A minor / la mineur / a-moll

Edited by
Manfredo Zimmermann

DOWANI International

Preface

Giovanni Battista Bononcini's "Divertimento da camera III" in A minor for treble (alto) recorder and basso continuo is a melodious work which, as its title suggests, is intended to delight listeners and players alike. The piece has been edited and recorded by Manfredo Zimmermann, professor of recorder at the Wuppertal Musikhochschule and a specialist in early music. Our volume allows you to learn the piece systematically at three different tempi with a professional accompaniment.

The CD opens with the concert version of each movement. After tuning your instrument (Track 1), the musical work can begin. Your first practice session should be in the slow tempo. If your stereo system is equipped with a balance control, you can, by turning the control, smoothly blend either the recorder or the harpsichord accompaniment into the foreground. The recorder, however, will always remains audible – even if very quietly – as a guide. In the middle position, both instruments can be heard at the same volume. If you do not have a balance control, you can listen to the solo instrument on one loudspeaker and to the harpsichord on the other. Having mastered the piece at slow tempo, you can practice the second and fourth movements at medium tempo. We have omitted the medium tempo for

the first and third movements, which are already relatively slow in the original. Now you can play the piece with accompaniment at the original tempo. At the medium and original tempos, the continuo accompaniment can be heard on both channels (without recorder) in stereo quality. All of the versions were recorded live. The names of the musicians are listed on the last page of this volume; further information can be found in the Internet at www.dowani.com.

In keeping with their style, the slow movements of this piece rely heavily on elements of improvisation. We have therefore included only the most essential embellishments and phrase marks. Players are invited to add trills, mordents, slurs and so forth at their own discretion. The same holds true, of course, for the realization of the figured bass (basso continuo or harpsichord), as can clearly be heard on the recording.

We wish you lots of fun playing from our *DOWANI 3 Tempi Play Along* editions and hope that your musicality and diligence will enable you to play the concert version as soon as possible. Our goal is to provide the essential conditions you need for effective practicing through motivation, enjoyment and fun.

Your DOWANI Team

Avant-propos

Le "Divertimento da camera III" pour flûte à bec alto et basse continue en la mineur de Giovanni Battista Bononcini est très mélodieux et procure du plaisir et du divertissement – comme le dit déjà son titre – non seulement aux auditeurs, mais encore au flûtiste. Manfredo Zimmermann, professeur de flûte à bec au Conservatoire Supérieur de Wuppertal et spécialiste dans le domaine de la musique ancienne, a édité et enregistré ce divertimento. Notre édition vous permet de travailler l'œuvre d'une manière systématique dans trois différents tempos avec un accompagnement professionnel.

Le CD vous permettra d'entendre d'abord la version de concert de chaque mouvement. Après avoir accordé votre instrument (plage n° 1), vous pourrez commencer le travail musical. Le premier contact avec le morceau devrait se faire à un tempo lent. Si votre chaîne hi-fi dispose d'un réglage de balance, vous pouvez l'utiliser pour mettre au premier plan soit la flûte à bec, soit l'accompagnement au clavecin. La flûte à bec restera cependant toujours audible très doucement à l'arrière-plan. En équilibrant la balance, vous entendrez les deux instruments à volume égal. Si vous ne disposez pas de réglage de balance, vous entendrez l'instrument soliste sur un des haut-parleurs et le clavecin sur l'autre. Après avoir étudié le morceau à un tempo lent, vous pourrez ensuite travailler le 2ème et le 4ème mouvement à un tempo modéré. Le

1er et le 3ème mouvement ne sont pas proposés dans un tempo modéré, car leurs tempos originaux sont déjà relativement lents. Vous pourrez ensuite jouer le tempo original. Dans ces deux tempos vous entendrez l'accompagnement de la basse continue sur les deux canaux en stéréo (sans la partie de flûte à bec). Toutes les versions ont été enregistrées en direct. Vous trouverez les noms des artistes qui ont participé aux enregistrements sur la dernière page de cette édition ; pour obtenir plus de renseignements, veuillez consulter notre site Internet : www.dowani.com.

Suivant le style de l'époque, les mouvements lents de cette œuvre laissent beaucoup de place à l'improvisation ; c'est pourquoi nous n'avons noté que très peu d'ornements et de phrasés. Chaque musicien peut ou doit ajouter ses propres indications (trilles, mordants, liaisons etc.). Cela concerne également la réalisation de la basse chiffrée (basse continue ou clavecin) – comme on l'entend bien sur notre enregistrement.

Nous vous souhaitons beaucoup de plaisir à faire de la musique avec la collection *DOWANI 3 Tempi Play Along* et nous espérons que votre musicalité et votre application vous amèneront aussi rapidement que possible à la version de concert. Notre but est de vous offrir les bases nécessaires pour un travail efficace par la motivation et le plaisir.

Les Éditions DOWANI

Vorwort

Giovanni Battista Bononcinis „Divertimento da camera III" für Altblockflöte und Basso continuo in a-moll ist sehr melodiös komponiert und soll – wie bereits der Titel sagt – sowohl dem Zuhörer als auch dem Spieler viel Vergnügen bereiten. Manfredo Zimmermann, Professor für Blockflöte an der Musikhochschule Wuppertal und Spezialist für Alte Musik, hat dieses Divertimento herausgegeben und eingespielt. Unsere Ausgabe ermöglicht es Ihnen, das Werk systematisch und in drei verschiedenen Tempi mit professioneller Begleitung zu erarbeiten.

Auf der CD können Sie zuerst die Konzertversion eines jeden Satzes anhören. Nach dem Stimmen Ihres Instrumentes (Track 1) kann die musikalische Arbeit beginnen. Ihr erster Übe-Kontakt mit dem Stück sollte im langsamen Tempo stattfinden. Wenn Ihre Stereoanlage über einen Balance-Regler verfügt, können Sie durch Drehen des Reglers entweder die Blockflöte oder die Cembalobegleitung stufenlos in den Vordergrund blenden. Die Blockflöte bleibt jedoch immer – wenn auch sehr leise – hörbar. In der Mittelposition erklingen beide Instrumente gleich laut. Falls Sie keinen Balance-Regler haben, hören Sie das Soloinstrument auf dem einen Lautsprecher, das Cembalo auf dem anderen. Nachdem Sie das Stück im langsamen Tempo einstudiert haben, können Sie den zweiten und vierten Satz auch im mittleren Tempo üben. Beim ersten und dritten Satz haben wir auf das mittlere Tempo verzichtet, da sie im Original schon relativ langsam sind. Anschließend können Sie sich im Originaltempo begleiten lassen. Die Basso continuo-Begleitung erklingt im mittleren und originalen Tempo auf beiden Kanälen (ohne Blockflöte) in Stereo-Qualität. Alle eingespielten Versionen wurden live aufgenommen. Die Namen der Künstler finden Sie auf der letzten Seite dieser Ausgabe; ausführlichere Informationen können Sie im Internet unter www.dowani.com nachlesen.

Da die langsamen Sätze dieses Werkes dem Stil entsprechend sehr stark auf improvisatorischen Elementen beruhen, wurden nur die nötigsten Verzierungen und Phrasierungen notiert. Der Spieler oder die Spielerin darf/soll gerne eigene Ergänzungen (Triller, Mordente, Bindungen usw.) hinzufügen. Dies gilt natürlich auch für die Ausführung des Generalbasses (Basso continuo oder Cembalo) – wie in der Aufnahme deutlich zu hören ist.

Wir wünschen Ihnen viel Spaß beim Musizieren mit unseren *DOWANI 3 Tempi Play Along*-Ausgaben und hoffen, dass Ihre Musikalität und Ihr Fleiß Sie möglichst bald bis zur Konzertversion führen werden. Unser Ziel ist es, Ihnen durch Motivation, Freude und Spaß die notwendigen Voraussetzungen für effektives Üben zu schaffen.

Ihr DOWANI Team

Divertimento da camera III

for Treble (Alto) Recorder and Basso continuo
A minor / la mineur / a-moll

G. B. Bononcini (1670 – 1747)
Continuo Realization: M. Zimmermann

DOW 2510

Giovanni Battista
BONONCINI

(1670 – 1747)

Divertimento da camera III
for Treble (Alto) Recorder and Basso continuo
A minor / la mineur / a-moll

Treble (Alto) Recorder / Flûte à bec alto / Altblockflöte

DOWANI International

Recorder

Divertimento da camera III

for Treble (Alto) Recorder and Basso continuo
A minor / la mineur / a-moll

I ②

G. B. Bononcini (1670 – 1747)

DOW 2510

4

IV ⑤

Giovanni Battista
BONONCINI

(1670 – 1747)

Divertimento da camera III
for Treble (Alto) Recorder and Basso continuo
A minor / la mineur / a-moll

Basso continuo / Basse continue / Generalbass

DOWANI International

Basso continuo

Divertimento da camera III
for Treble (Alto) Recorder and Basso continuo
A minor / la mineur / a-moll

I

G. B. Bononcini (1670 – 1747)

Tempo giusto

DOW 2510

II

4

IV

Presto assai

8

Vivace

Vivace

DOW 2510

ENGLISH

DOWANI CD:

- Track No. 1

- Track numbers in circles

- Track numbers in squares

  - slow Play Along Tempo
  - intermediate Play Along Tempo
  - original Play Along Tempo

| 1 | - tuning notes |

⬤ - concert version

- Additional tracks for longer movements or pieces

- **Concert version:** recorder and basso continuo

- **Slow tempo:** The recorder can be faded in or out by means of the balance control. Channel 1: recorder solo; channel 2: harpsichord accompaniment with recorder in the background; middle position: both channels at the same volume

- **Intermediate tempo:** basso continuo only

- **Original tempo:** basso continuo only

FRANÇAIS

DOWANI CD :

- Plage N° 1

- N° de plage dans un cercle

- N° de plage dans un rectangle

  - tempo lent play along
  - tempo moyen play along
  - tempo original play along

| 1 | - diapason |

⬤ - version de concert

- Plages supplémentaires pour mouvements ou morceaux longs

- **Version de concert :** flûte à bec et basse continue

- **Tempo lent :** Vous pouvez choisir – en réglant la balance du lecteur CD – entre les versions avec ou sans flûte à bec. 1er canal : flûte à bec solo ; 2nd canal : accompagnement de clavecin avec flûte à bec en fond sonore ; au milieu : les deux canaux au même volume

- **Tempo moyen :** seulement l'accompagnement de la basse continue

- **Tempo original :** seulement l'accompagnement de la basse continue

DEUTSCH

DOWANI CD:

- Track Nr. 1

- Trackangabe im Kreis

- Trackangabe im Rechteck

  - langsames Play Along Tempo
  - mittleres Play Along Tempo
  - originales Play Along Tempo

| 1 | - Stimmtöne |

⬤ - Konzertversion

- Zusätzliche Tracks bei längeren Sätzen oder Stücken

- **Konzertversion:** Blockflöte und Basso continuo

- **Langsames Tempo:** Blockflöte kann mittels Balance-Regler ein- und ausgeblendet werden. 1. Kanal: Blockflöte solo; 2. Kanal: Cembalobegleitung mit Blockflöte im Hintergrund; Mitte: beide Kanäle in gleicher Lautstärke

- **Mittleres Tempo:** nur Basso continuo

- **Originaltempo:** nur Basso continuo

DOWANI - 3 Tempi Play Along is published by:
DOWANI International Est.
Industriestrasse 24 / Postfach 156, FL-9487 Bendern,
Principality of Liechtenstein
Phone: ++423 370 11 15, Fax ++423 370 19 44
Email: info@dowani.com
www.dowani.com

Recording & Digital Mastering: Wachtmann Musikproduktion, Germany
CD-Production: MediaMotion, The Netherlands
Music Notation: Notensatz Thomas Metzinger, Germany
Design: Andreas Haselwanter, Austria
Printed by: Zrinski d.d., Croatia
Made in the Principality of Liechtenstein

Concert Version
Manfredo Zimmermann, Treble (Alto) Recorder
Mechthild Winter, Harpsichord
Steffen Hoffmann, Cello

3 Tempi Accompaniment
Slow:
Mechthild Winter, Harpsichord

Intermediate:
Mechthild Winter, Harpsichord
Steffen Hoffmann, Cello

Original:
Mechthild Winter, Harpsichord
Steffen Hoffmann, Cello